PETER PORTER

The Cost of Seriousness

1978

OXFORD UNIVERSITY PRESS

OXFORD LONDON NEW YORK

Oxford University Press, Walton Street, Oxford OX2 6DP

OXFORD LONDON GLASGOW NEW YORK
TORONTO MELBOURNE WELLINGTON CAPE TOWN
IBADAN NAIROBI DAR ES SALAAM
KUALA LUMPUR SINGAPORE JAKARTA HONG KONG TOKYO
DELHI BOMBAY CALCUTTA MADRAS KARACHI

British Library Cataloguing in Publication Data

Porter, Peter
    The cost of seriousness.
    I. Title
    821   PR9619.3.P57   77–30533

    ISBN 0–19–211880–3

PRINTED IN GREAT BRITAIN BY
THE BOWERING PRESS LTD, PLYMOUTH

The Cost of Seriousness

To Janet.
with love from
Charlie.
Christmas '79.

For Sally McInerney

CONTENTS

ACKNOWLEDGEMENTS

ACKNOWLEDGEMENTS are due to the editors of the following periodicals in which some of these poems first appeared : *Ambit, Aspect, Encounter, New Review, New Statesman, Outposts, Pick, Poetry Australia, Quadrant, Thames Poetry, The Times Literary Supplement,* and *TR.* Several others were first read in radio programmes broadcast by the BBC and ABC.

Many of the poems in this book were written while I was receiving a grant from the Literature Board of the Australia Council. This help proved vital to me, and I should like to thank the Council for its generous support.

Peter Porter

OLD FASHIONED WEDDING

It was for this they were made,
The great present of their childhood
Kept unopened, the hard rules obeyed
And the grudged honey of being good :
A pure reward,
Better for being stored,
And, reached at last, seeming like the sea
Stretching after a dream of ice toward
The edge of reluctance properly.

So that the stunned moment now
When talk falls in the bright marquee
Is an elevation of hope, the drinks a vow
Naming everything which is to be;
And after this
The subtly twinned kiss
To start a carnal journey, and the night
Offering shining emphasis
Like crystal gifts emboldening the light.

To which the cynical, caught up
In the flurry of guy ropes let down,
And crushed flowers in delicate cups,
Pay tribute as sexual clowns.
After this huge
Joke, a terrible deluge
The speeding innocents know nothing of,
Mad hours, silence, subterfuge
And all the dark expedients of love.

AT RAMSHOLT

The harvest is in early. Across the paddock,
where we raise the bull's head with mimic
bellows, through the salt-dead trees and thatcher's
rushes, yachts navigate on seeming land.

This is the Deben, not the Mekong, but a sail
curves round a copse; masts for Woodbridge
crowd three degrees of the horizon, edging
a painterly Dutch sky. Clouds are curdling.

A golden rain of ladybirds falls in the lap
of Suffolk. Drought has driven the wasps mad,
they butt the kitchen glass. A cucumber,
like Masolino's Satan, rears under grass.

To townsmen everything is like something
from a book—most noticeably in this
made landscape. The swan on the canal,
with nine cygnets, is the Home Fleet, 1936.

Ezekiel in church : shall these bones live?
The pheasants live another month and then
go plumply down. A nightingale sings
politely through the dangerous summer.

THE PICTURE OF NOBODY

We are always being framed somewhere. A camera, an eye
Of memory is recounting inches along from the pea-trellis,
The cement-block fence, the rotary clothes-line : a leg
Is not quite where it seemed and an arm forward on the thigh
Strikes a posture more aggressive than the smiling face.

Then, beside the church where a clapped-out pigeon fell
To be picked up by a not-very-poor-looking Italian—was
She standing higher on the steps, or perhaps just out of sight
To the left? The Hotel de Beurs was surely closer to the canal,
The photograph should smell of cleansing and dark cloths.

Years after, another presence makes itself felt, someone
Who wasn't there when we bought the angle-poise lamp
And were snapped in the street, a shape which vanished
From the wharf-side beer garden and the Japanese bridge
Over an English river—now he seems so very like me.

A sentimental assumption. We put up our own coordinates,
The bars of our prison. Her own picture the doppelganger,
She was already haunting those September stones with
Her death, just as at seven the teeth stick out which
Later slope in, rodent-like. The wave freezes at its crest.

Bring the coordinates together to get us out of unhappiness.
We are in limbo. And his picture is quite clear now.
He will move to the new album, the later, more hopeful
Photos over the same ground. Three cats on top of each other
Behind a grille in Venice, or a window of star-shaped ice-creams.

No wonder there are ghosts. What we leave behind is deadly.
The melody is played, a poisonous, long-lasting scent
Circles the garden. Spring again. Our friend has borrowed
A loved face to bring the bad news to the still living :
There is nobody else in the picture, yet fear looks out.

3

WAITING FOR RAIN IN DEVON

Rain here on a tableau of cows
might seem a return to everyday—
why, you can almost poach
the trout with your hands,
their element has so thickened !
Something has emerged from dreams
to show us where we are going,
a journey to a desolate star.
Come back, perennial rain,
stand your soft sculptures in our gardens
for the barefoot frogs to leap.

THE ORCHID ON THE ROCK

Two hundred yards from the house
Where the sounds of trees commence
With water always in descent
From the hundred veins of the creek,
The orchid rears its dozen necks
On a cushion of self : not scent
But a colourless colour, so intense
It eats the light, brings us up close.

Perhaps fifty years' battening on
Its own dead limbs have sent
Those roots like rivets into the rock—
The air brings stories of other lives :
Lemons returned to wildness, leaves
A hundred feet overhead which mock
The ferns, a fallen cedar bent
To the creek to kiss the sun.

Our sounds are the noise of feet
Unplugging from the grassy bog
And words at the service of botany—
We hush now for the daring orchid.
Art meets the world at an awkward
Angle, offering no harmony
Of fact and feeling—the sniffing dog
Butts through lantana foxing fruit.

The orchid blooms in perfect nowhere;
We go home to our electrified fort
To create relationships.
From the verandah, viewing the river

On its civilising course, a fever
Of loneliness encroaches, grips
The mind. A clarinet has caught
The empty evening unawares.

THE CHARNEL HOUSE, ST LEONARD'S, HYTHE

One of us, the prettiest,
would like a skull for an ash tray.
We who have flesh round our skulls
and can imagine the pain of dying
are proper company
for these generations of the sexes.

One is soon to be dead herself,
another wishes that he were,
self-indulgent, waiting for a voice . . .
A calm night after a blistering day,
the evening quiet with disappointment
and the apertures of death.

A bad opera on the radio,
proving that words and notes
make little difference,
and everywhere inside the summer room
the brilliant and disgusting skulls
with never a thought of names.

A PORTRAIT BY GIULIO ROMANO

Dear long-dead lady,
what was it like in the world
of Aretine's postures?
The highlights of your beauty
are a blond tombeau
but you are in a cage.

Your white skin and your red
velvet dress—the uniform of love!
They have shaken out boxes
before your eyes, they have formed
letters on your lips, and held
your legs apart for the state.

We are wrecked on red dreams.
Eloquence is quickness,
the flying to extremes—
your pose and prettiness
are to keep off endings,
the highmindedness of hell.

POEM WAITING TO BE TRANSLATED

I have tried to stop drinking
because it makes me sadder
and upsets my bladder,
but evenings come on
and doubtless something unnameable is done
in some unlighted place.

Why not remember the heroes
of hard situations,
those who answered inquisitors
in fresh parables,
whose lyrical rejoinders
are assembled here
in memorial Penguins?

But not all are dead.
I met someone today
who said her years up to thirty
had been undoubtedly happy,
and I have seen with my own eyes
a dissident poet eating whitebait
and joking from the corner of his mouth.

O the lungs of poets
and their hunch backs—
They are looking for the chalk
of apotheosis, tutorial rooms
of some exchange agreement
where the homesick specialist
says hello to a lime tree.

There the moon walks over
the Marches and murders
small lives by stagnant lakes,

fireflies swing round the ears
of fishermen setting out,
the landscape is stoic
and policed by malaria.

At this point in our history,
everything is Un-English!
I say to the Japanese professor
who wants to know about Mateship :
we have reached a pluralism
of culture in our language,
and I should like my wise instances
subsidised and printed
with generous margins.

After the funeral of the drunken poet,
the busybody dogs disperse
on some business of their tails
and the dead walk the land
casting no shadow.

THE LYING ART

It is all rhetoric rich as wedding cake
and promising the same bleak tears
when what was asked for but not recognized
shows its true face after a thousand breakfasts.

This, not Miss Moore's disclaimer, tells me
why I too dislike it. It is paid to distract us,
to tell the man disappointed by his mother
that he too can be a huge cry-baby.

Think of its habit of talking to gods
but saying only pastoral things. Real pain
it aims for, but can only make gestures,
the waste of selling-short, the 'glittering'.

I want you to be happy, you say,
but poetry brings in childhood on its horse,
the waves of parrots and the Delphic eyes,
and is never there when the scab is picked.

Music gets the better of it, since music is all lies.
Lies which fill the octave. Chromatic space
in verse turns out to be the ego's refractions,
truth always stained by observation.

So this argument goes in cut-up prose,
four lines to each part. I will not say
metric or stanzas or anything autonomous,
but keep to discontent, a nearly truthful art.

And what has this to do with poetry? Inroads
into rhetoric. The ugly and the disappointed
painting their faces with words; water showing
God's love to the beautiful—no way of changing.

11

Then we might as well make the best of
dishonesty, accept that all epithalamiums
are sugar and selfishness. Our world
of afterwards will have no need of lies.

THE EASIEST ROOM IN HELL

At the top of the stairs is a room
one may speak of only in parables.

It is the childhood attic,
the place to go when love has worn away,
the origin of the smell of self.

We came here on a clandestine visit
and in the full fire of indifference.

We sorted out books and let the children
sleep here away from creatures.

From its windows, ruled by willows,
the flatlands of childhood stretched
to the watermeadows.

It was the site of a massacre,
of the running down of the body
to less even than the soul,
the tribe's revenge on everything.

It was the heart of England
where the ballerinas were on points
and locums laughed through every evening.

Once it held all the games,
Inconsequences, Misalliance, Frustration,
even *Mendacity, Adultery* and *Manic Depression.*

But that was just its alibi,
all along it was home,
a home away from home.

Having such a sanctuary
we who parted here
will be reunited here.

You asked in an uncharacteristic note,
'Dwell I but in the suburbs
of your good pleasure?'

I replied, 'To us has been allowed
the easiest room in hell.'

Once it belonged to you,
now it is only mine.

AN ANGEL IN BLYTHBURGH CHURCH

Shot down from its enskied formation,
This stern-faced plummet rests against the wall;
Cromwell's soldiers peppered it and now the death-
       watch beetle has it in thrall.

If you make fortunes from wool, along
The weeping winter foreshores of the tide,
You build big churches with clerestories
       And place angels high inside.

Their painted faces guard and guide. Now or
Tomorrow or whenever is the promise—
The resurrection comes : fix your eyes halfway
       Between Heaven and Diss.

The face is crudely carved, simplified by wind;
It looks straight at God and waits for orders,
Buffeted by the organ militant, and blasted
       By choristers and recorders.

Faith would have our eyes as wooden and as certain.
It might be worth it, to start the New Year's hymn
Allowing for death as a mere calculation,
       A depreciation, entered in.

Or so I fancy looking at the roof beams
Where the dangerous beetle sails. What is it
Turns an atheist's mind to prayer in almost
       Any church on a country visit ?

Greed for love or certainty or forgiveness ?
High security rising with the sea birds ?
A theology of self looking for precedents ?
       A chance to speak old words ?

Rather, I think of a woman lying on her bed
Staring for hours up to the ceiling where
Nothing is projected—death the only angel
      To shield her from despair.

AN EXEQUY

In wet May, in the months of change,
In a country you wouldn't visit, strange
Dreams pursue me in my sleep,
Black creatures of the upper deep—
Though you are five months dead, I see
You in guilt's iconography,
Dear Wife, lost beast, beleaguered child,
The stranded monster with the mild
Appearance, whom small waves tease,
(Andromeda upon her knees
In orthodox deliverance)
And you alone of pure substance,
The unformed form of life, the earth
Which Piero's brushes brought to birth
For all to greet as myth, a thing
Out of the box of imagining.

This introduction serves to sing
Your mortal death as Bishop King
Once hymned in tetrametric rhyme
His young wife, lost before her time;
Though he lived on for many years
His poem each day fed new tears
To that unreaching spot, her grave,
His lines a baroque architrave
The Sunday poor with bottled flowers
Would by-pass in their mourning hours,
Esteeming ragged natural life
('Most dearly loved, most gentle wife'),
Yet, looking back when at the gate
And seeing grief in formal state
Upon a sculpted angel group,
Were glad that men of god could stoop

To give the dead a public stance
And freeze them in their mortal dance.

The words and faces proper to
My misery are private—you
Would never share your heart with those
Whose only talent's to suppose,
Nor from your final childish bed
Raise a remote confessing head—
The channels of our lives are blocked,
The hand is stopped upon the clock,
No-one can say why hearts will break
And marriages are all opaque :
A map of loss, some posted cards,
The living house reduced to shards,
The abstract hell of memory,
The pointlessness of poetry—
These are the instances which tell
Of something which I know full well,
I owe a death to you—one day
The time will come for me to pay
When your slim shape from photographs
Stands at my door and gently asks
If I have any work to do
Or will I come to bed with you.
O scala enigmatica,
I'll climb up to that attic where
The curtain of your life was drawn
Some time between despair and dawn—
I'll never know with what halt steps
You mounted to this plain eclipse
But each stair now will station me
A black responsibility
And point me to that shut-down room,
'This be your due appointed tomb.'

I think of us in Italy :
Gin-and-chianti-fuelled, we
Move in a trance through Paradise,
Feeding at last our starving eyes,
Two people of the English blindness
Doing each masterpiece the kindness
Of discovering it—from Baldovinetti
To Venice's most obscure jetty.
A true unfortunate traveller, I
Depend upon your nurse's eye
To pick the altars where no Grinner
Puts us off our tourists' dinner
And in hotels to bandy words
With Genevan girls and talking birds,
To wear your feet out following me
To night's end and true amity,
And call my rational fear of flying
A paradigm of Holy Dying—
And, oh my love, I wish you were
Once more with me, at night somewhere
In narrow streets applauding wines,
The moon above the Apennines
As large as logic and the stars,
Most middle-aged of avatars,
As bright as when they shone for truth
Upon untried and avid youth.

The rooms and days we wandered through
Shrink in my mind to one—there you
Lie quite absorbed by peace—the calm
Which life could not provide is balm
In death. Unseen by me, you look
Past bed and stairs and half-read book
Eternally upon your home,
The end of pain, the left alone.

I have no friend, or intercessor,
No psychopomp or true confessor
But only you who know my heart
In every cramped and devious part—
Then take my hand and lead me out,
The sky is overcast by doubt,
The time has come, I listen for
Your words of comfort at the door,
O guide me through the shoals of fear—
'Fürchte dich nicht, ich bin bei dir.'

THE DELEGATE

In the garden (it was always a garden)
there is the punishment of remembrance.
I pray you love, remember. And quote me
the many things which might come to you
on your own death bed.
                    I was there
even in our worst hour—the wreaths
and the mis-named name competing with
the other mourners' flowers upon
the crematorium slabs. I am divided
into an infinity of myself, pieces
for everywhere—especially that damp day,
that insistence on seriousness.
We shall never be so serious again.
But this frees you for levity today,
and perhaps a little licenced selfishness.
Take this gift of despair—what can
a ghost give but remembrance and
forgetfulness in the right proportions?

Never to puff up those sloping headlands
watching the children ahead negotiating
the lanes of the wide bay : never
the afternoon sun straining
the bedroom light to a tint distinctly
like gin : never more the in-flight panic,
refusing to see omens in our food
or the number of letters in the month.
                 These *nevers*
are just parts of my docility
as I go back. I am always receding,
my ambition is to accomplish
non-existence, to go out and close the door
on ever having been.

                              I am doing it in death
as I did in life—but it's so hard.
I cannot forget unless you remember,
pin down each day and weighted eye
with exact remorse. After fifteen years'
convergence, now we may draw apart
and face our different exits.

So I am your delegate
at the screaming hours : I walk alone
among the plains of hell. We dream here
in the skin of our deeds : such changes
as the schoolgirl saw in her body
are metamorphoses of the gods.
                              First I went back,
a quick change in the early morning
with my blood running into frost.
Now the reduction is set at smaller things—
I may even become the healthy strider
or flamenco dancer, but I must reduce, reduce,
become so small that I escape the eye
of god. There is no peace here, or on earth.
                              You will know
how the mind works at poems, feels ideas
as tissue—but, alas, the ceremony here
is different. I am not what you remember,
the snapshots in time and sunshine,
nor even the angry and accusing face
at breakfast, the suddenly delivered tone
of hope along a Venetian calle on a Sunday—
                              I am made fiction
by my needs : the brain changing in the garden
to a bush of thorns, a dream looking for
its dreamer, murder always at the end
of every vista. A letter now, headed

'Malcontenta, Orto Chiuso', a puff-adder's face
as I prop myself against the dying mirror
viewing disgust with satisfaction.
                              Breaking an egg-cup,
learning to give up, crying at the sight
of a withered seahorse pinned to the wall :
all those afternoons of hope and all those gardens,
no wonder I cannot escape now.
                              After a year in office,
your delegate has found this court
a place of ashes and the matches
played by moonlight cruel games.
But I have an immense truth to give you—
In the end, we are condemned
only for our lack of talent.
                              There is no morality,
no metered selfishness, or cowardly fear.
What we do on earth is its own parade
and cannot be redeemed in death. The pity
of it, that we are misled. By mother,
saying her sadness is the law, by love,
hiding itself in evenings of ethics,
by despair, turning the use of limbs
to lockjaw.
                              The artist knows this.
He is being used despite himself. The truth
is a story forcing me to tell it. It is not
my story or my truth. My misery
is on a colour chart—even my death
is a chord among the garden sounds.
                              And in this garden, love,
there will be forgiveness, when
we can forgive ourselves. 'Remember me,
but ah forget my fate.' Tell me like music
to the listeners. 'I would not know her in that dress.'

The days I lived through change to words
which anyone may use. When you arrive
I shall have done your work for you.

                    Forgetting will not be hard,
but you must remember still. Evenings
and mad birds cross your face,
                    everything must be re-made.

A LECTURE BY MY BOOKS

You cannot write tonight. We own all
the words you will ever need to make a shape
of permanence. But they were used by
men who felt along the lines
to life. We are dead
who kept the watch for you while your landscapes burned,
we stand like stele
on the road to hell. Fear us.

And market us in dreams. We
are the finished phrase, the play of gesture stopped
before one death. See this gasping soul
declare a total library of meaning
less than a nerve end,
Anacreon's grave a house
of roots and the reaching out goodbye
your only poem.

From *Julius Caesar* and the laws
of aspic hardening, the heart will
snatch a vocabulary—
'I just want to be dead'—and all the novels
fry tonight. What did
poor Carrington find in her shotgun barrels?
Words for ending words,
the picture of nobody there.

In this garden of categories
a night rose withers—
it was the spume of Rilke,
words lying on the carpet where a planet
winters and the dapper genius
welcomes god to his
own twentieth century : a rich tapis
for tongue-tied democracy.

To be the actuaries of hope,
not so many graveyards of trees but gestures
in a terrible silence—
To be recognized,
a man, a woman
and a relationship. But the cat
has seen through their plan. He knows they have only
printed their hearts. He reads knees.

Here are the lines of a last conspiracy.
Listen to our words,
there are no others. Can you write now?
The brain's a neologism of rare aspect
but it isn't quite music.
We've sat on your walls and heard
the moon cry for the dead, poor centaurs,
poor Humpty Dumpties.

SCREAM AND VARIATIONS

When I came into the world I saw

My face in my mother's blood
and my father crying where he stood.

A garden where a girl teased a man,
a man listened to a girl complain,
a boy wondered what a man could mean.

A house where children's voices rang,
where tiredness lived for each evening,
where a wife needed to be among
friends, and kids and a husband stayed wrong.

A party smiling for a photograph—
one choking on the length of his life,
another ready to raise tears for a laugh,
one death harvested with a knife,
doors closing on a broken belief.

An ecologist painting Doomsday
for ten million watchers; tragedy
in the newspapers and poetry
in the schools; all style in a lie
and truth a shapeless story;
the lark ascending a poisoned sky.

My coffin in an unknown place
among enemies and the police;
my daughters trying to please
me in dreams with their replies;
a tear belonging to my wife ablaze
in the darkness of widowhood; peace
in her voice but only death's applause.

Myself in the world is all there was.

'IN THE NEW WORLD HAPPINESS IS ALLOWED'

No, in the New World, happiness is enforced.
It leans your neck over the void and the only
recourse is off to Europe and the crowded hearts,
a helplessness of pasta and early closing days,
lemons glowing through the blood of Acre.

It is the glaze of galvinism—why are there
so many madmen in the street? O, my countrymen,
success is an uncle leaving you his fruit farm.
The end of the world with deep-freezes, what if
your memories are only made of silence?

In one year he emptied the sea of a ton of fish.
He wasn't one to look at the gardens of Greenslopes
and wish they were the verdure of the Casentino.
Living with the world's reserves of ores,
no wonder our ruined Virgils become democrats.

Masturbation has been known in Europe too
and among the gentiles. Why did nobody say
that each successful man needs the evidence
of a hundred failures? There is weekend leave
from Paradise, among the caravanning angels.

Here's a vision may be painted on a wall :
a man and a boy are eating with an aborigine
in a boat; the sun turns up the tails of fish
lying beside the oars; the boy wipes surreptitiously
the bottle passed him by the black man.

Rain strums the library roof. The talk tonight
is 'Voluntary Euthanasia'. Trying to be classical
can break your heart. Depression long persisted in
becomes despair. Forgive me, friends and relatives,
for this unhappiness, I was away from home.

THE COST OF SERIOUSNESS

Once more I come to the white page of art
        to discover what I know
        and what I presume I feel
about those forgettable objects words.
        We begin with penalties :
The cost of seriousness will be death.

Not just naming death again to stoke fires,
        but thinking of suicide
        because life or art won't work
and words trying to help, Mallarmé-like,
        undefine themselves and say
things out of the New Physics : self-destruct !

Which is why the artist must play, but if
        he does he mustn't rule-change
        and say, 'Unless you agree
to Pound's huge seriousness I shan't go
        on living, and meanwhile we
are an elite of experimenters,

to whom someones in the city must pay
        homage, dons give neat memos
        and our correspondents pile
up hagiography in magazines—'
        A public worthy of its
artists would consist of whores and monsters.

So, to turn impatience into anger
        and want to punish slow minds
        or walk through our museums
with a clock ends up as despair or a
        professorship in exile,
the world as solipsistic as ever.

At which you may ask (ungentle reader)
        why does he avoid the point?
        After great vindication
coming through B Flat this way will never
        be the same, and so the earth
changes while we stand by a grave and mourn.

Yes, but the earth stays the same too, greeting
        leaves and their sons each season
        just seasonally; the boat
for Venice idles at the green-furred wharf
        carrying the body of
the composer Grimace (Ettore),

as timetable-conscious as if it had
        on board a scientist who
        could make a food crop of grass,
and I have come no closer to my goal
        of doing without words, that
pain may be notated some real way.

Seriousness—ah, *quanta pena mi*
        costi! I note from a card
        that hills are dyed purple by
a weed named Paterson's Curse. That is in
        New South Wales. The dead may pass
their serious burdens to the living.

31

THREE TRANSPORTATIONS

1 *Gertrude Stein at Snail's Bay*

I am Miss Stein
and this bay is mine

I am Miss Stein (pronounced Steen)
and this sea is green

Americans do not like
European pronunciation

I live in Europe because Americans
do not like Europeans

I do not live in America
because Europeans do not like Americans

I am in Australia because
I hear you have an opera
and I am searching for snails

I am not here to buy your paintings

I am in Snails Bay to find snails

Although there are no snails in Snails Bay
there are buses behind me
and children in front of me
and sea in front of the children

They tell me this is Arbor Day

No, I do not drop my aitches

Nothing can be done in the face
of ordinary unhappiness

Above all, there is nothing to do in words

I have written a dozen books
to prove nothing can be done in words

A great artist may fall off an inner alp
but I will not roll down this gentle bank

I would not give a cook book for his alp

I have a message for the snails
of New South Wales

You will never know
which of you is Shakespeare

Yes, I am a disagreeable old woman
who talks selfishly and strangely
and writes down words in a peculiar order

It is to prevent unhappiness escaping
and poisoning the world

How do you define
the truth, Miss Stein?

A snail has not the right to say
it will or won't : it must obey

With the buses and the children and the sea
I have nothing to do

I am an observer,
I observe the blue and you

I see an immense rain
washing pebbles up the beach
and evacuating misery

The plane for America is a sort of star

2 *Piero di Cosimo on the Shoalhaven*

Through a banksia's cone the fire passes,
Aphorisms of the deities of time.
Here on a broad river's side, my glasses
Squandering the sun, I put rhyme
Into paint, Vulcan's and Venus's trespasses.

On a rock orchid, the roundness and gloze
Of a lapith's bum ! Men hauled cedars
From these forests before their blood froze,
Making a camp for gods—our leaders,
We sighed, as we looked inside the rose.

My eggs boil on the electric stove—
Reincarnation of madness : one
Takes a mainline trip to Comfort Cove,
Another paints the rain forest in the sun,
A murder and a mating in a grove.

Drongo the dog is barking at a thing
Washed up on a sandbank by the tide—
A nymph, a suicide, something decomposing
Which his nose loves, and at its side
The mercenaries of life converging.

Up river the water skiers puff and plane;
I could not imagine more blended beasts.
The gods are husbanding our pain
Like all good settlers—the men of feasts
Will come, a Medicean super-strain.

Neither Adam nor Jesus ever laughed
But the serious earth is quite hilarious.
This is Eden as the cattle go past
The electric fence; the faces are so various
Of flower and shadow, which will last?

Only work can save us from night coming.
Newly-planted trees attest the faith.
On its dorsal, a monster is drumming
Messages for the new world—each wraith
Is a spirit of old Europe slumming.

Here.I put a duck-billed wallaby,
A swimming jackass, abo-centaur:
So old a place has so much still to see,
There must be ghost traps. Shut the door
On dying, become a lamenting tree.

3 *The Boccherini Music Camp*

The widower as wooer—
no more awkward gesture
since Creation!

'Your refuge is your work',
but Signior Boccherini
is too fluent—he's forgotten
how many quintets he's written,
and he put a son through college
on a minuet.

As I said to your Arts Reporter
asking about myself
and Scarlatti and other
erstwhile exiles in Iberia :
'Out of Italy we come,

35

great talent, little room;
the hatred is for family.'

That portrait down in Melbourne,
scratching at the belly of invention—
you see me in servitude to sex and Prussia.
Each confrontation seems
another Right Wing Coup,
my cello as large as Spain.

Now for the Muse of Mittagong—
I like your lady viola-players.
I would not call this a sexy country
but they have pollen in their hair
and down upon their lips.

When I start an allegro
it's planned like those washing programmes
right through to the spin-dry.
In my view I should be called
Haydn's husband.

You can make sounds of sadness
but when the music stops
the heartless world will whistle—
every defeat stays on
as an examination question.

Do my children love me?
I doubt that any of my quavers
would bail me out—
I have been far away
all my life.

The call of strings through upland wattles,
my music recognizes me—
there is no time left
to outplay misery.

EVENSONG

Coming upon them suddenly,
the memorials of oh so long
ago, as tourists will do,
after a coffee and brioche,
the horseman galloping
in rain, the big dog
and the top dog locked
behind fine ironwork,
just as Ruskin saw them,
and hardly knowing they
were tombs, instances
of what was never far
from our own heads—
death outlasting love.

The scale, the Scala, the puns
of churches—that grinner
tip-toeing in brocade
and those martyrs' doilies
for their little-boned hands :
morbidity—see the river
run through its castled bridge
and a leaf jump to it
from a tree near us,
a career in air and water,
and from the top row
of the amphitheatre
the Alps chatter like
our gin-rinsed teeth.

Then to miss the way,
confidently stalking
past a prison—a real one
made of stone not days—

and take hours to find
the doors of truth, the old
benign image of hope
which couldn't fool us,
sky outside like the walls
of candle-smoked churches,
no other harmony for the night
but the separation of
sleep going on forever.

TO VENETIA'S SHORES HAVE COME

They say this state is sinking
and that its waters are a health hazard,
but boys dive into the canal
from the Fondamenta Bragadin,
the same boys every morning.

The cats are clean and hold convocations
on the silvery fish of charity.

What the Signore would give
to be back in Mann's and Corvo's days
when he might have taken a gondola
or imagined Ruskin on the Zattere.

An unlikely text rises as he walks
in sunshine to San Bastian,
'the state killed our mothers, they were depressed'—
To bring the world to your parish church
and lie there at the end,
that's a noble monstrance!

For the gods of the jewel-box
have come down from the clouds :
a favourite insight watching
the knife-flecked waves beyond San Vio,
the Pope to the Bishop of Gibraltar,
'Then I am in *your* diocese.'

The Signore joins those
who have had a vision in Venice—
The Last Days walking on the waters
in applauded levitation
and into his ears these words,
'Yours is the first and only death.'

'A city built by strong men
in the image of their mother.'
Not even this is the whole truth,
the corny stuff is better,
'I am afraid to visit the Lido
for fear I should die there.'

The light is moving away from Europe
and the Signore hasn't as much time as Goethe
who, after all, found the grave of Consul Smith.
Lost on a dark sea, he keeps in mind
a few relics—a toe, a claw of Venus
who ate her own placenta, an Eastern city
painted on the falling sun.

LOOKING AT A MELOZZO DA FORLI

And in this instance we think of you, God,
You beard above all things,
Canceller of every fact except death,
Looking down on your grand intercession,
Orthodox, like the artist's vision,
Helpless helper of time and promise.

But we do not get closer to love.
The angel's admonitory finger
And the lily of greeting tell Mary only
That the clock in her womb is ticking,
That she will come sooner to sorrow.

And I can see too in the structures
Of church and family another death.
We are entered by the spirit
And thereafter comes such rich despair—
Sermons of the penis, oddities by the seashore
Where towns have sunk, letters lost
In the mumblings of a drunken alphabet.

What is Mary kneeling on? A yoke,
A box for Miss Plath's mad bees,
A stiff pew for a protestant sunday?
In one revolution her body shows
Disquiet, reflection, inquiry, submission, merit.

These shapes Melozzo put on a wall
Fade like the dove-voiced poet
Into a high wood of darkness.
From his flat-bottomed cloud, God observes
Earthly love and sadness, saying
After all, this is only a language of gestures.

Yes, Mary, you are an actor in a play
Whose dénouement is now to be spoken.
I rehearse the lines myself to your angel—
The action is beginning, blessèd is the Virgin
Who shall be the mother of death.

THE PAINTERS' BANQUET

They came with their gifts of the senses
And of the groves planted for them by God
In the retina; they knelt by sandy waters
And saw a violin shore, a fronded region
Of high responding light, rosella afternoon;
They gossiped in laps, lay under umbrellas
Of the tumid shade; they told colours
In every story. When the pelican glided,
They overcame light, where the daisy unpeeled
They saw graveclothes. There were many
With eyelashes like Veronese's fans,
Others sat solitary as meat on a plate
Waiting for heaven to happen. Change,
Said some, was the way of their world,
Animals answering the call of light
Under Hyperion's crag. But, said several,
It is the unchanging we celebrate,
Sirocco afternoons, gods hard-pressed
By their abstract eyes. Dangerous modes
In all weather when obsessionals walk
To a favourite spur above the land—
Below them kingdoms boil and they find
Twisting paths through middle space.
This is the sumptuous gallery of those
Who have eaten the world. Oh the ochre,
Burnt siena, the pulverising red
Which rocks have earned from the sun—
In little spaghetti-making towns,
The dead artificers' creations burn
All sophistry from pilgrims' eyes.

It was a wonderful party to be at.
We write our thank-you letters
In the world's far-reaching galleries.

Who will clean up now? All the water
In the reservoirs won't remove the stain
From Golgotha. We think back instead :
Little Andrea has drawn a sheep
With a bright stone upon a smooth-faced rock.
Lucky for him a Medici is passing.
Soon the banquet will be set again.

'TALKING SHOP' TANKA

Looking at six books
of poems, painfully and
    yet so slovenly
produced over thirty years,
I notice one well-wrought phrase.

My friends are subtle,
their insights into colonels,
    keys and plasticine
shame my generalisations
and Horatian pleasantries.

After toothache or
sexual rejection, the
    epics are supposed
to come : instead, sexual
rejection and toothache recur.

Why are Catullus,
Baudelaire and Neruda
    so much translated?
The task is impossible,
the intention praiseworthy!

On the steps after
the Memorial Service
    for Auden, five men
talking—the legendary
Establishment in full view!

Loss or gain, the change
in Western self-consciousness
    may be measured by
the distance between Rameau's
Nephew and Beethoven's.

We are too many
is also what the Muses
       said to Apollo.
The only domain with room
for everyone is Limbo.

       The Church, the Army
and the Law are all too hard—
       nowhere to pack off
a useless son but the Arts,
preferably Poetry.

       All those brainy girls
editing Meredith—no
       wonder the Muses
come to us as sex pots, and
Hermes wears a mackintosh.

       Lope de Vega's
daughter, prop of his old age,
       was carried off by
a hidalgo. The plots of
his plays had long schemed revenge.

       Goethe pleases all
Germans and Wystan Auden,
       but Schiller via
Schubert touches our hearts with
his 'Schöne Welt, wo bist du?'

       'Since she whom I loved
hath paid her last debt to Nature
       and to hers, and my
good is dead . . .' I can't go on,
I share death not faith with Donne.

SCHUMANN SINGS SCHUBERT

An old woman,
so the record sleeve denotes,
is singing of death
in a young world—
the glow of a wedding dress,
the shine on a coffin.

German Art,
how it penetrated
our dull afternoons!
Vienna's sons
journeying across carpets
of millstreams and graveyards.

'So lasst mich scheinen . . .'
One day Mignon will get
over the Alps
to America or Australia
and offer them death
to sweeten their late songs.

NON PIANGERE, LIÙ

A card comes to tell you
you should report
to have your eyes tested.

But your eyes melted in the fire
and the only tears, which soon dried,
fell in the chapel.

Other things still come—
invoices, subscription renewals,
shiny plastic cards promising credit—
not much for a life spent
in the service of reality.

You need answer none of them.
Nor my asking you for one drop
of succour in my own hell.

Do not cry, I tell myself,
the whole thing is a comedy
and comedies end happily.

The fire will come out of the sun
and I shall look in the heart of it.

A BRAHMS INTERMEZZO

The heart is a minor artist
hiding behind a beard.
In middle age
the bloodstream becomes a hammock
slowing down for silence—
till then, this lullaby,
arpeggiated thunder
and the streams running
through Arcadia. I, too,
says the black-browed creature
am in this vale of sweetness,
my notes are added to eternity.

A SCARLATTI SONATA

When I see her hand on an envelope
my own hand shakes. While I am explaining
the ritual to my heart, she is writing
to the stars. As plain rules add to richness,
our rare arrival covers manuscripts.
These are clothes to wear before our father.

I stare at my own hand and at the marks
it makes on paper. Untrained fingers
shape the cursive style of love. Her hands
are fitting out the gods as well as
writing letters. Fewer notes than usual
from the harpsichord, each one a sun.
Her voice will speak of love
but her hands must prove it in the world.

L'INCORONAZIONE DI POPPEA

To have known personally the demon
he who sits singing in the fire
('the occupational disease of poets is frivolity')
to experience suffering real as a colour
and hear it praised (green, green, O green)
to wait at the hospice for death
one hand searching for another
a continuous melody, a story
this was worth being born for
the world's unfairness still playing
we have invented love, it licks us
(*pur ti miro, pur ti godo*)
the great bridges bow, the streets appear
the marriage of never to now
against any justice or reason
unfaithful, steadfast, forever
(Bacchus in his barge, an end to ending)
the golden eyes of the phoenix
the coronation of fire

ROMAN INCIDENT

The two of us, tired after a night
of quarrelling and making love
to make up quarrels and not quite
succeeding, first found the airline
in a Roman street and made our bookings,
then moved in a slightly drunken way
through the boring Via Veneto
to the Borghese Gardens. So far, so much.
An ice-cream eaten, a path adopted—
she must simply lie down and sleep
in the grass and I who couldn't sleep
stay there beside her. A woman sleeping
makes me lonely : I saw love in her face
and I had seen love die before,
so I left her and walked across other lovers
to the Gallery. All that awful
Carravagiesque paint and Cardinal Scipio
straight from the movies. At last,
a marvellous Carpaccio of a whore,
a quick look at my watch, thinking of
her lying there in the grass,
resolved to make one circuit and then leave—
but here I came upon a picture,
Dosso Dossi's *Melissa*, apotheosis
of the watching female and her autumn shades.
Left hand lower corner a labrador
ready to nuzzle to his master
in stockbroker Surrey and in the woods,
russet with the ferns of terra firma,
the enclosed bodies of men reassuming
their uncanted shapes. Garrulous
as a Fabian hostess, the lady ties
your looking with her colours—
the painter has borrowed Titian's later dyes

for pure frivolity. Armorial death
enchants when this Melissa looks :
frozen jibes from long-running
civil epics out of Italy, Ariosto's suspense,
Tasso's cracks on the head—Dossi warms them
in his hand. Life is a spell
and when we wake from it
the animals of our senses stand
with us in play-power paradise.
Visit Melissa's extra-mural zoo,
you'll find yourself hiding in shrubbery
when a truthful woman summons you.
Standing frozen before her on a plinth
of grief and awkwardness, I tried to cry,
to force water from my eyes, so that
Melissa might turn me back to manhood—
that, I said, is what I want. Magic, fortune, love :
the luck to be kissed and smiled on
no matter what ridiculous wizard
corks up my heart. To mother,
wife and all the sultry dead I prayed,
lead me to the enchantress whose one kiss
undoes the tactless misery of self.
            When I got back
to our flattened patch of grass, she'd gone
and I was desperate. Of a sudden
I heard her call my name and saw her body
approaching on the path. Her sleep had eased her
so we walked to lunch and an afternoon's
sightseeing via Pantheon and Forum,
ahead of us the night and our hotel.

UNDER NEW MANAGEMENT

After a discipleship of plain days,
The first born of the bourgeoisie,
It is disturbing to be offered this coast
For one's training as Messiah,
Albeit (as the careful programme says)
The faithful will be few and the heathen
Prominent—the change is quite important,
There is to be a seascape out of dreams
And a city founded where tears fell.

Congratulations have filtered down through fear :
It might have been finished, all the words
Laid on that coffin for the fire. Not that
Reports show any alteration yet—capering
Creatures dance undisturbed, the Natural Histories
Keep their gods. No, in this ministry
Expect to find insurance and small print,
Miracles being where a higher syntax reigns,
Masters of the dormitory of graves.

But, as in a chorus by Euripides,
We speak of other instances—the nightingale
Among the lines of village washing,
The idiot with his windmill arms—
These are a species of true fiction
Which cities burned for or a river turned—
Give them to Helen for her civic rape
Or a Baptist figure scrambling ashore
To be Athens, Florence and the cliffs of mind.

The world, not just a section of the bowel,
Is under new management. Call it
A time of hope, that will not be wrong,
But say of it that the sleeper finds

A daytime dream : strangeness persists,
As when hibiscus wavers on the path
And shows a face of love and several words
To mask it. Poets and warriors seek the supreme
But we have here the very quotidian.

The occasion for a sermon is at hand
(Other than love letters which speak
Into a mirror)—the place, a landscape
Under Winter Hill. I saw the river
A ribbon of death and the willows weeping
To the grass—now it's a bland decalogue,
Music for a while. Time ends amazingly
Among the notes, sinopia of Eden,
And worms are for forever in the Campo Santo.

This long way round, this garrulous hopefulness
Is how we veterans speak. Younger callings
Assume the pulpit, making love by harangue.
Our gospel (I must not call it mine)
Is to praise the seconds into minutes,
Making the minutes hours, and to let them all
Dance while the light lasts—trite under
Its poetry, hardly a philosophy,
But a change of programme in the blood.

I dedicate my years in the field to one
Body only, she of the catalytic eyes.
Whether Dionysus or some other hard man
Of the hills will lead us, we shall be
Caught up in the evening's enterprises.
As god of this place, my own savannas,
I praise her and I lead her forth
Into a published garden. She'll be silver
By mine and by the stars' true light.